FOOD CHAINS AND WEBS

What Are They and How Do They Work?

Andrew Solway

Rourke

Publishing LLC

Vero Beach, Florida 32964

www.rourkepublishing.com

PHOTO CREDITS: p. 28: Anthony Bannister/Gallo Images/Corbis; p. 16: Lester V. Bergman/
Corbis; p. 15: Carlos Cazalis/Corbis; p. 21: Alexander V. Chelmodeev/ istockphoto.com;
p. 6: Brandon D. Cole/Corbis; p. 43: Corbis; p. 5: Nicole Duplaix/Getty Images; p. 35:
Steve Geer/istockphoto.com; pp. 12, 18, 27, 30, 34: istockphoto.com; p. 32: Vebjorn
Karlsen/istockphoto.com; p. 41: Evgenia Lazareva/istockphoto.com; p. 40: Linda & Colin
McKie/istockphoto.com; p. 39: Michael Melford/Getty Images; p. 9: NASA; p. 38: Ed
Parker/EASI-Images/CFWImages.com; p. 22: Mike Parry/Minden Pictures/FLPA; p. 31:
Svetlana Prikhodka/istockphoto.com; p. 14: Horst Puschmann/istockphoto.com; p. 11:
Andy Rouse/Getty Images; p. 42: Andy Sacks/Getty Images; p. 25: Dmitriy Smaglov/
istockphoto.com; title page, p. 19: Boris Tavasov/istockphoto.com; p. 26: Vasiliki Varvaki/
istockphoto.com; pp. 17, 29: Visuals Unlimited/Corbis; p. 24: Sandra vom Stein/
istockphoto.com; p. 20: Terry Whittaker/FLPA; p. 8: Judy Worley/istockphoto.com;
p. 4: Norbert Wu/Minden Pictures/FLPA.

Cover picture shows a grizzly bear hunting for salmon.
[Sandra vom Stein/istockphoto.com].

Produced for Rourke Publishing by Discovery Books
Editors: Geoff Barker, Amy Bauman, Rebecca Hunter
Designer: Ian Winton
Cover designer: Keith Williams
Illustrator: Stefan Chabluk
Photo researcher: Rachel Tisdale

Library of Congress Cataloging-in-Publication Data

Solway, Andrew.
  Food chains and webs : the struggle to survive / Andrew Solway.
      p. cm. -- (Let's explore science)
   ISBN 978-1-60044-601-6
   1. Food chains (Ecology)--Juvenile literature. I. Title.
   QH541.15.F66.S65 2008
   577'.16--dc22
                                            2007020001

CONTENTS

CHAPTER ONE

OTTERS, URCHINS, AND KELP

We often hear about living things being endangered. Sometimes the plant or animal is becoming **extinct**, or dying out. Often we have never heard of the animal or plant that is in danger. Does it matter if it dies out?

The story of the sea otter shows what can happen if a species disappears from an area. In the past, sea otters lived all along the west coast of North America.

Sea otters often use tools to get their food. They put a stone on their stomach and use it to break open shellfish and other food.

Sea otters lived along the east coast of Asia, too. In the eighteenth century, trappers began to hunt sea otters. They wanted the otters' thick, silky fur. Soon, otters began to disappear from the coast. By 1911, there were less than 2,000 otters left in the world.

AMAZING FUR

Some sea mammals such as seals and whales have a thick layer of fat under the skin. This helps keep out the cold. Otters do not have this fat layer. They have only fur. To keep them warm, the fur is very thick. One square inch of fur (2.5 sq. centimeters) contains one million hairs. This is ten times the number of hairs on your head.

Purple sea urchins like these live all along the west coast of America. Their main food is giant kelp.

Bald Patches

The sea otters live in forests of brown seaweed. This seaweed is called giant kelp. When otters in an area died out, "bald patches" appeared in the kelp. These patches were caused by sea urchins. Sea urchins eat kelp. But otters eat sea urchins. They keep down the number of sea urchins.

PURPLE TEETH

It is easy to tell when a sea otter is eating lots of purple sea urchins. Its teeth turn purple! And though you can't see it, the otter's bones are purple, too.

Luckily, sea otters did not die out. Now, they are protected. They have come back to many areas. As they come back, the kelp starts to recover.

Food Chains and Webs

Sea otters, sea urchins, and kelp are connected. The connection is through food. These kinds of connections are called food chains. They often occur between living things in an **environment**.

Other living things are connected to this food chain. Sea otters eat things besides sea urchins. And kelp forests feed creatures besides sea urchins. Many living things are connected together in a food web.

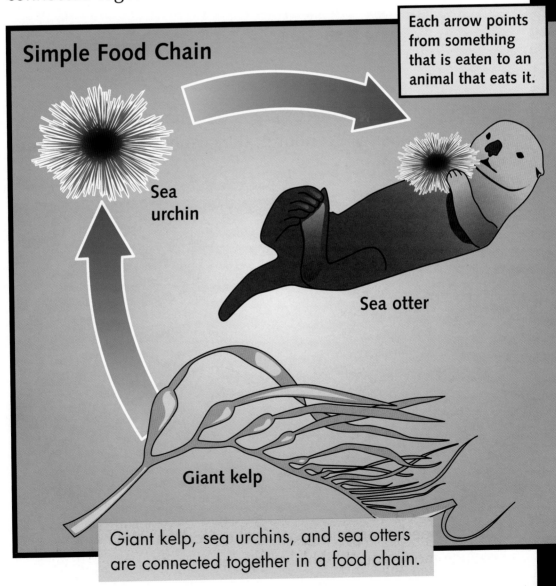

Simple Food Chain

Each arrow points from something that is eaten to an animal that eats it.

Sea urchin

Sea otter

Giant kelp

Giant kelp, sea urchins, and sea otters are connected together in a food chain.

CHAPTER TWO

ALL ABOUT ENERGY

Food chains and food webs are about **energy**. All living things need energy. Without it, they cannot grow, or move, or produce young.

Animals need energy to grow and reproduce. Wolf spiders produce many young, which they carry on their backs.

As we will see in the next chapter, plants get their energy from the Sun. They use light energy to make their own food.

SUN POWER

Earth gets less than a 2 billionth of the energy the Sun makes. This is still a lot of energy. But just how much is that? Let's put it in terms we understand. It would take 440 million large power plants to make as much energy as Earth gets from the Sun.

Animals cannot make their own food. They have to eat to get energy. Some eat plants and others eat animals. Some eat both animals and plants. Ultimately, all the food animals eat comes from plants. And plants get their energy from the Sun. So all living things get their energy from the Sun.

Energy Losses

Plants use only a tiny amount of the energy that comes from the Sun. Some energy goes back into space. Some warms the land and oceans. Only 1 or 2 percent of the energy from the Sun is absorbed by plants.

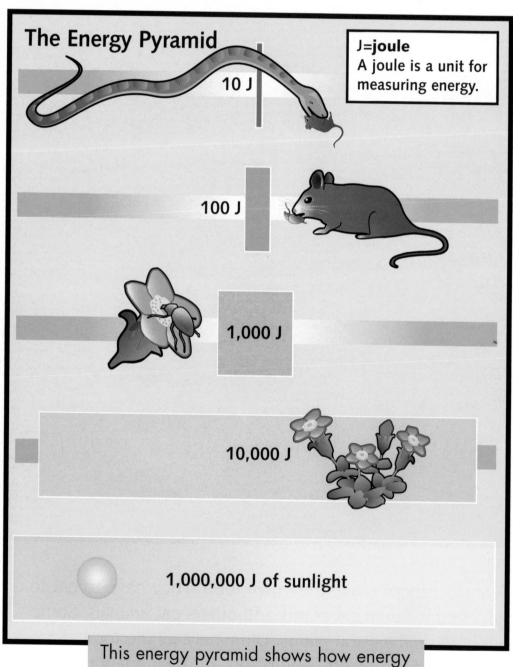

The Energy Pyramid

J=joule
A joule is a unit for measuring energy.

10 J

100 J

1,000 J

10,000 J

1,000,000 J of sunlight

This energy pyramid shows how energy is lost at each stage in a food chain.

Plants do not turn all this energy into new growth. Only about a tenth of the energy becomes plant material. So animals that eat plants get only a tenth of the energy that the plant got from the Sun.

Animals like this cheetah use a lot of the energy from their food for moving around.

Like plants, animals lose a lot of the energy they get from plants they eat. They turn only about a tenth of the energy they get from plants into meat. So animals that eat other animals get only a thousandth of the energy that the plant got from the Sun. Each stage of the food chain has less energy than the one before it. Because of this, there are more plants than plant-eating animals. And there are more animals that eat plants than animals that eat meat.

CHAPTER THREE

PRODUCERS

A food chain or web shows how energy moves from one group of living things to another. Think of a mouse. A mouse gets the energy it needs from eating grass and seeds. If the mouse is eaten by a snake, its energy moves up the food chain to the snake.

The starting points in any food chain or web are the living things that make their own food. These are called **producers**. On land, green plants are the main producers.

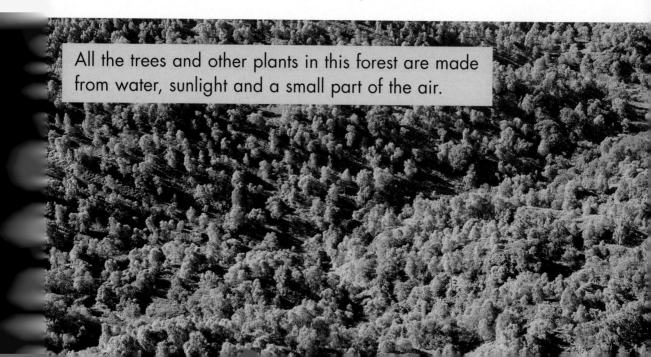

All the trees and other plants in this forest are made from water, sunlight and a small part of the air.

Green plants make their own food. This process is called photosynthesis. To do this, they need sunlight, the gas carbon dioxide, and water. With the energy from sunlight, plants can combine water and carbon dioxide to make glucose (sugars). The sugars are the plant's food.

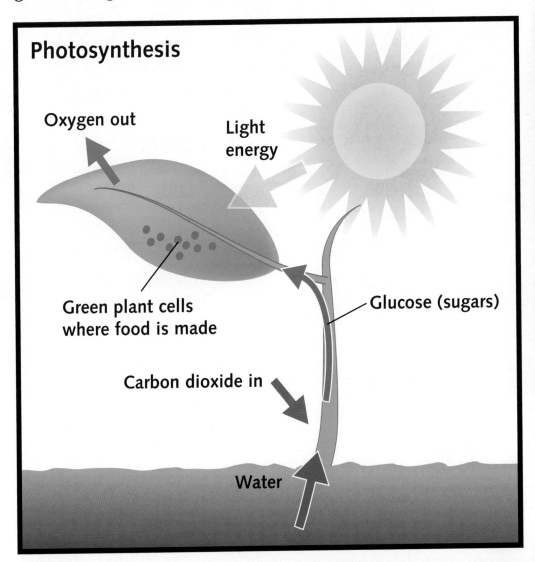

Photosynthesis

Oxygen out

Light energy

Green plant cells where food is made

Glucose (sugars)

Carbon dioxide in

Water

BIGGEST LIVING THINGS

Plants are the world's largest living things. Sequoia trees are probably the largest of the plants. The biggest of these trees is nearly 275 feet (84 meters) tall. It weighs more than 2,000 tons (2,032 tonnes).

Seaweeds are not always green, like land plants.
They can be red, or brown like this kelp.

Producers in the Oceans

In the ocean, there are no green plants to make food.
Seaweeds such as kelp are one ocean producer. The ocean's
main producers are **plankton**. Plankton are simple creatures
that float on ocean currents. They can be plants, animals, or
bacteria. Plant plankton is called **phytoplankton**.

Phytoplankton make food through photosynthesis, like green
plants. And like green plants, they need sunlight to make
food. So phytoplankton are found close to the ocean surface.

Although tiny, phytoplankton make more food than land plants. Two-thirds of all the photosynthesis on Earth is due to phytoplankton.

RED TIDES

Where ocean conditions are right, phytoplankton do well. There can be billions of phytoplankton in a bucketful of water. When there are so many of them, they turn the water green, brown, or red.

Kinds of Plant Plankton

There are many kinds of phytoplankton. The most common are **diatoms**, blue-green **algae**, and d**inoflagellates**.

PIRATE HATS AND SNOWFLAKES

Diatom skeletons can have many different shapes. There are round diatoms that look like doughnuts. Some diatoms look like long boats. Other diatoms look like snowflakes. There are even diatoms that have three corners. They look like pirate hats.

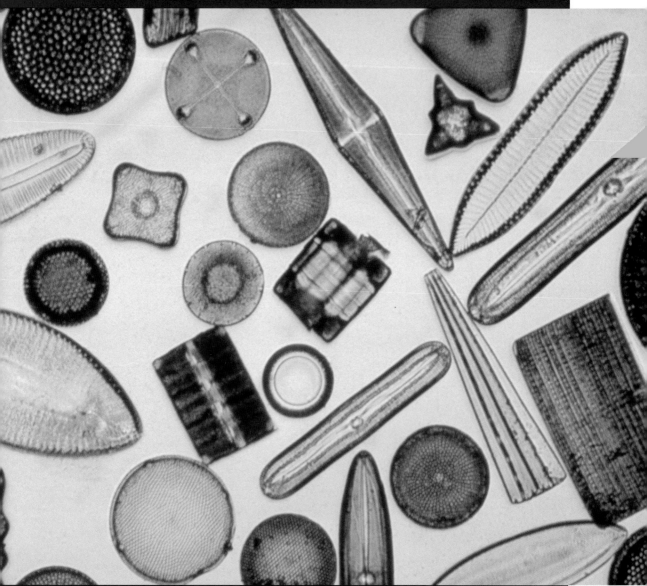

Diatoms have beautiful clear skeletons. They look as if they are made of glass. They are the most common plankton in cooler seas. Blue-green algae are actually a bacteria. They join together in long strings, sheets, or hollow balls. Large numbers of them can turn the sea blue-green.

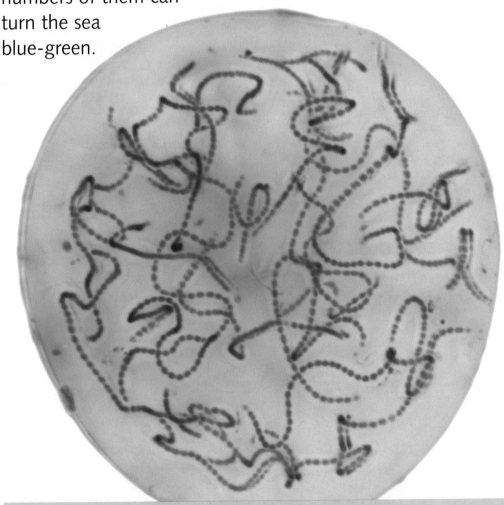

Blue-green algae are the oldest of all living things. There have been blue-green algae on Earth for over 3500 million years.

Dinoflagellates are found in tropical waters. They are common around coral reefs. They are also found in freshwater. All dinoflagellates have a long, whiplike "tail." This is called a flagella. Whipping it from side to side, they move through the water.

CHAPTER FOUR
CONSUMERS

Any living thing that needs to eat food is a consumer. All animals are consumers. So are many microscopic creatures.

Many consumers eat plants or parts of plants. They are called **primary consumers**. They are also known as **herbivores**. Animals such as cows, horses, elephants, deer, and rabbits are grazers. They eat grass and the leaves from bushes and trees.

Hummingbirds need lots of energy to keep themselves alive. Sugary nectar is a high-energy food that keeps them going.

OCEAN HERBIVORES

The ocean has many herbivores. Many of these primary consumers feed on phytoplankton. One group is zooplankton. Zooplankton are animal plankton. Other herbivores include small fish, squid, sea urchins, and krill. The shrimplike krill are found in the cold oceans. And sea urchins, as you know, feed on coral reefs and kelp.

Other animals eat seeds and fruit. Among these are squirrels, bats, sparrows, finches, and parrots. Hummingbirds, butterflies, and bees eat the nectar from flowers. Soil animals, such as grubs and worms eat plant roots. All these animals are primary consumers.

Secondary Consumers

Next come the **secondary consumers**. These animals eat primary consumers. Some of these are large **predators** such as lions, wolves, crocodiles, and eagles. They may eat animals bigger than they are. Some lions, for example, kill and eat water buffalo. The buffalo weigh twice as much as the lions do.

Weasels catch very large prey. They are deadly killers. A single bite to the back of a rabbit's neck kills it at once.

FIERCEST PREDATOR?

Which animal is the fiercest predator? You could measure the fierceness of a predator by the size of its prey. Then weasels would top the list. Weasels often hunt rabbits. Rabbits can weigh nearly ten times as much as the weasel.

Other secondary consumers eat animals smaller than they are. Shrews, moles, birds, and most lizards eat insects. Some larger animals also eat insects. Anteaters and sun bears are two examples. These animals have to eat many insects. An anteater, for instance, may eat as many as 30,000 insects every day.

Mantises are also fierce predators. They eat all kinds of small creatures, including spiders, like this one.

Tertiary Consumers

Some animals are called tertiary consumers. This means they eat secondary consumers. Tertiary consumers are often the "top predators" in a food chain. This means that no other animals eat them.

A great white shark leaps out of the water, catching a seal in its jaws. A shark is a tertiary consumer.

An area has only a few top predators. To see why, think about the energy pyramid. (See page 10). It has many plants at the bottom. But only some of the energy from those plants gets turned into new animals. This means there will be fewer primary consumers. And there will be even fewer secondary and tertiary consumers.

LONG FOOD CHAINS

In the ocean, food chains can be long. They may have a stage beyond tertiary consumers. For example, plant plankton is eaten by animal plankton. These creatures are then eaten by small fish. The small fish are eaten by a big fish. The big fish could then be eaten by a shark or a whale.

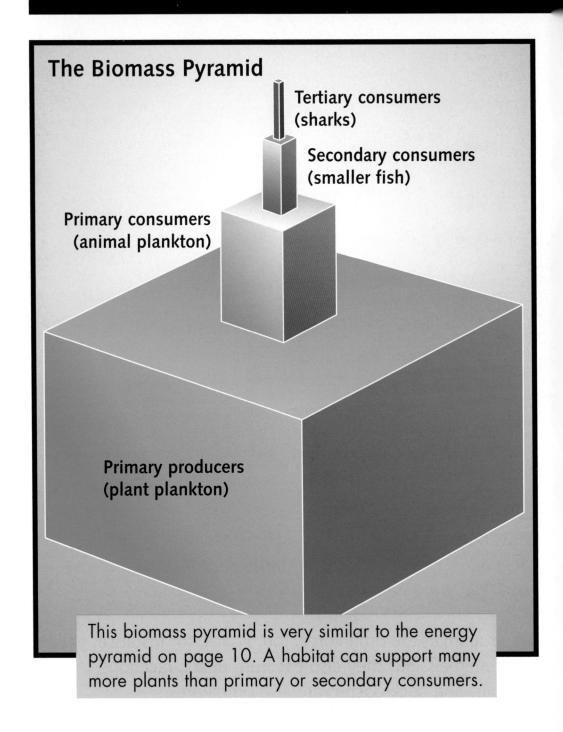

The Biomass Pyramid

Tertiary consumers
(sharks)

Secondary consumers
(smaller fish)

Primary consumers
(animal plankton)

Primary producers
(plant plankton)

This biomass pyramid is very similar to the energy pyramid on page 10. A habitat can support many more plants than primary or secondary consumers.

Bears, like this grizzly, enjoy catching salmon or other fish. However, they also eat plant food such as fruit and honey.

Omnivores

Most humans are not just primary consumers or just secondary consumers. We eat both plant food and animal food. We are **omnivores**.

Other animals are omnivores, too. Foxes, for instance, eat other animals. But they also eat fruit. Bears, raccoons, seagulls, and cockroaches are also omnivores.

Some omnivores are **scavengers**. This means they eat food that other animals have left. Hyenas, for example, eat the remains of animals that have been killed by predators. They have strong jaws and teeth. With them, they can crunch through bones.

Hedgehogs eat mainly slugs, snails, beetles, and worms, but they also eat fruit.

PARASITES

Parasites are animals or plants that live on or inside other animals or plants. They are consumers. The mistletoe plant is a parasite. It lives on other plants. Roundworms are also plant parasites. Fleas and tapeworms are also parasites. They sometimes feed on humans.

CHAPTER FIVE
DECOMPOSERS

When we make and eat a meal, there is nearly always waste. When we go to the toilet, we rid our bodies of waste. This waste comes from the food we have eaten. Imagine none of this waste was cleared up. It would soon cover the Earth. **Decomposers** are nature's way of removing and recycling waste food.

The mold on this orange is a kind of fungus, called *penicillium*. The fungus grows by drawing **nutrients** from the orange.

DECAY IN THE GARDEN

To see decay at work, start a compost pile. A compost pile is made of garden and kitchen waste. Decomposers get to work on the leaves, dead flowers, grass cuttings, and vegetable peelings. Soon they begin to rot. After a few months, the garden waste has turned into rich compost. Compost is "food" for the garden soil. It will help plants grow faster.

Decomposers make things rot. They break down plant and animal waste—everything from dead trees to insect droppings. Decomposers turn these into **minerals** and other simple substances. These enrich the soil and help new plants grow.

Big Decomposers

Bacteria and fungi are important decomposers. They break down the chemicals in living things. They turn them into nutrients for plants. Some larger animals also help the process of decay.

These include earthworms, slugs, and many insects. Slugs eat dead and rotting plant material on the ground. Earthworms eat the soil itself. Insects such as maggots and some flies eat dead animals. Other insects such as termites and beetles tunnel in wood. Dung beetles gather animal droppings. They bury the waste as food for their young.

These animals have important jobs. They break up waste. This makes it easier for the real decomposers to get to work.

Dung beetles gather animal droppings and roll them into a large ball. Then they lay their eggs along with the ball of dung. When the eggs hatch, they feed on the animal dung.

OCEAN CLEANERS

In the ocean, most animal waste falls to the ocean floor. Here creatures such as crabs, starfish, and sea urchins feed on the waste. Other animals do not wait for the waste to fall to the bottom. Barnacles, mussels, and many other creatures are filter feeders. They stay in one place. There, they filter small pieces of food out of the water.

Fungi are among the most important decomposers in woodland. These poisonous woodland fungi are called fly agaric.

Little Decomposers

Waste material is broken up into small pieces. Then small decomposers go to work. There are thousands of kinds of bacteria in the soil. Different types of bacteria feed on different chemicals in the soil. The waste that they produce is simple chemicals such as **nitrates**. These are important plant nutrients.

WHEN THE GOING GETS TOUGH...

One of the toughest substances in living things is lignin. It makes wood hard and strong. Most bacteria and fungi cannot break down lignin. However, some microbes can soften it. These microbes are actinomycetes. They are similar to bacteria and grow in long threads, like fungi.

Fungi are also important decomposers. The mushrooms and toadstools that we think of as fungi are not the main part of the fungus. The "body" of a fungus is a network of fine threads spread through the soil.

Bracket fungi often grow on the trunks of old ard dead trees.

CHAPTER SIX

FITTING IT ALL TOGETHER

We have seen how different plants and animals are connected to each other through food chains. But very few things are part of a single food chain.

KELP FOREST FACTS

Giant kelp grows very fast. It is one of the fastest growing of all living things. It can grow more than 300 feet (90 m) in a year. This is important. Many creatures live in the kelp forest. Scientists found 23,000 animals around the roots of just five kelp plants.

Let's look again at the food chain in Chapter 1. This chain connected kelp, sea urchins, and sea otters. Sea urchins eat kelp. But other animals, such as sea snails and crabs, do too. So kelp is part of more than one food chain. At the other end of the chain, the sea otter eats more than sea urchins. It also eats clams and other kinds of food. As with the kelp, sea otters are part of other food chains. Kelp, sea urchins, and sea otters are part of a food web. Each food web involves many plants and animals.

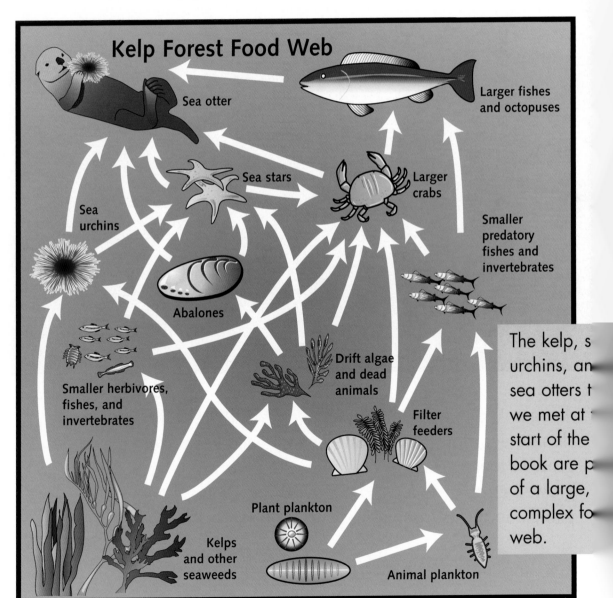

Kelp Forest Food Web

Sea otter

Larger fishes and octopuses

Sea stars

Larger crabs

Sea urchins

Smaller predatory fishes and invertebrates

Abalones

Smaller herbivores, fishes, and invertebrates

Drift algae and dead animals

Filter feeders

Plant plankton

Kelps and other seaweeds

Animal plankton

The kelp, s urchins, an sea otters t we met at start of the book are p of a large, complex fo web.

Think about the food chains and webs in different places. Clearly some places can support a richer mix of living things than others. The diversity (richness) of an area in a region depends on which plants can live there. And which plants can live there depends on the climate.

Woodlands grow where the climate is not too cold, and not too dry. In this kind of climate, large numbers of plants can grow.

A region's climate is its average weather. Places with a warm climate get more of the Sun's energy each year. More plants grow in these areas. Rainfall also affects which plants can grow. Desert areas are dry. They cannot support many plants. So these areas are less rich in life.

The amount of plant life that can grow in an environment is called the **productivity** of that environment.

Deserts are areas where the climate is very dry. Without water, the land can support very few plants.

THE PRODUCTIVITY OF AN ENVIRONMENT

The graph below shows the productivity of different environments. Some are o
land. Some are in the ocean. Rainforests are the most productive land areas on
land. Estuaries (river mouths) and coral reefs are the most productive water are

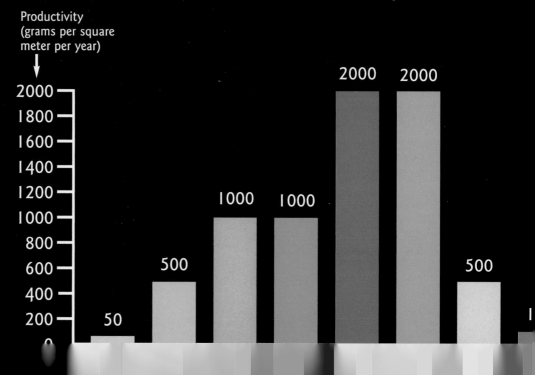

Productivity
(grams per square
meter per year)

2000
1800
1600
1400
1200
1000
800
600
400
200
0

2000 2000

1000 1000

500

50

500

Simple Webs

There are many different food webs in the world. Some are simple and include only a few **species**.

Desert food chains are often simple. Desert plants such as cactuses are the desert producers.

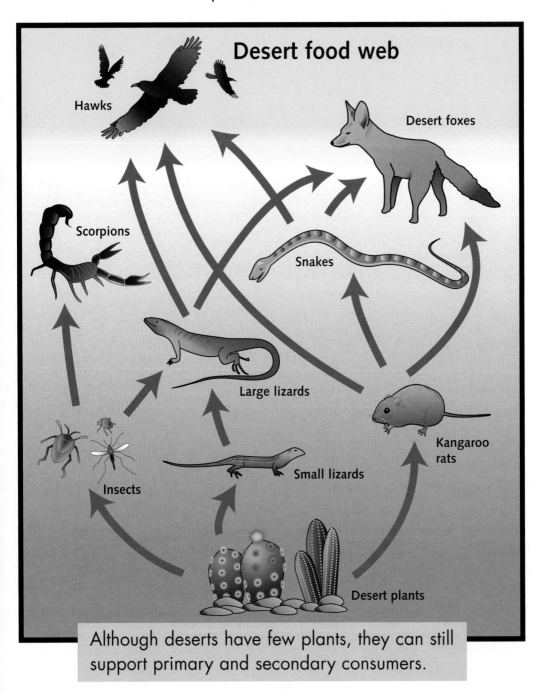

Desert food web

Hawks

Desert foxes

Scorpions

Snakes

Large lizards

Small lizards

Insects

Kangaroo rats

Desert plants

Although deserts have few plants, they can still support primary and secondary consumers.

A simple food web is found in the Antarctic Ocean. There, shrimplike krill eat plant and animal plankton. Fish, seabirds, penguins, seals, and whales eat the krill. Then, top predators such as toothed whales eat seals, penguins, and squid.

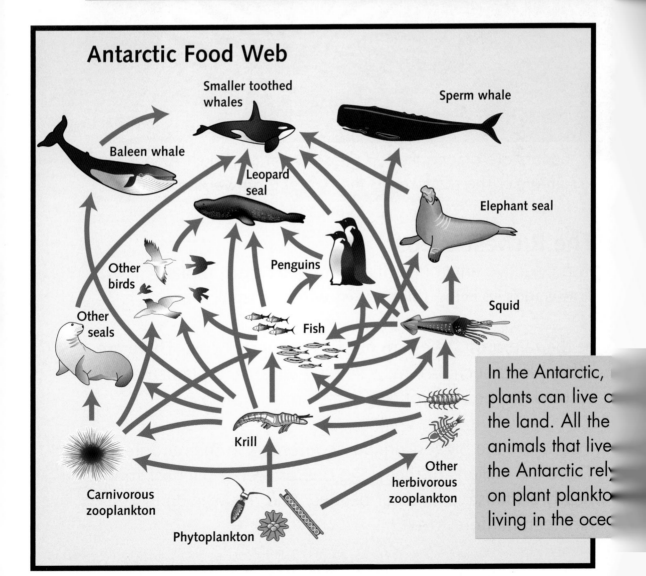

Antarctic Food Web

Baleen whale

Smaller toothed whales

Sperm whale

Leopard seal

Elephant seal

Other birds

Penguins

Squid

Other seals

Fish

Krill

Carnivorous zooplankton

Phytoplankton

Other herbivorous zooplankton

In the Antarctic, plants can live o the land. All the animals that live the Antarctic rel on plant plankto living in the oce

Jaguars are among the top predators in the South American rainforest. The rainforest is the richest food web on Earth.

The Richest Webs

In productive environments, food webs are complex. Thousands of living things exist within a small area.

In the rainforest, trees are not the only producers. There are other plants such as ferns, climbing vines, and plants called epiphytes. The roots of epiphytes grow in the air.

Insects are the biggest primary consumers in the rainforest. There are millions of them. On one project, a scientist found nearly a thousand kinds of beetles. And this was on just nineteen rainforest trees!

Secondary consumers include other insects, birds, snakes, lizards, and mammals such as anteaters and sloths. The top predators are jaguars, **caimans**, and eagles. The connections between all these living things are complex.

SUMMER FEAST

In some regions, food supplies vary. There may be plenty of food at one time of the year. At another point, there may be very little. For instance, the Arctic has plenty of food in the summer. But this is not true in winter. Animals such as **caribou** and many birds come to the Arctic during summer. They take advantage of the summer feast.

CHAPTER SEVEN

SHIFTING WEBS

Food webs change. They change as the environment changes. Imagine a group of plants dies out. Animals that feed on the plant must find other food to eat. Or maybe a new animal has come into an area. It competes with the animals already living there. These changes often affect the whole food web.

Often animals have to survive in difficult conditions. These cattle In Queensland, Australia, are competing for food in the same area.

NEW SPECIES

At times, people have brought animals or plants to areas where they did not belong. This can have awful effects on an area's food web. For example, rabbits were taken to Australia in the 1700s. They have since spread across the continent. Some areas are now overrun with rabbits. The rabbits damage both farm crops and the environment.

A group of orcas swimming off the coast of Alaska. Orchas often hunt in small groups known as pods.

The kelp forest web is an example of how food webs change. In recent years, sea otter numbers in Alaska have fallen. This happened because orcas (killer whales) started eating them. In the past, the whales ate mainly seals. But as seal numbers fell, the whales turned to sea otters for food.

Humans have changed food webs in many parts of the world. The biggest changes to the webs are caused by habitat destruction. We have destroyed forests, grasslands, and wetlands to grow crops and build cities and towns. Many living things have died out because of these changes.

Humans have changed the habitat in many parts of the world in order to grow food. These wheat fields in East Grand Forks, Minnesota, were once rolling grasslands.

CHANGING CLIMATE

Climate change is affecting food webs throughout the world. Many coral reefs are struggling to survive because the water has become too warm for them. At the other end of the world, polar bears are starving. The Arctic ice is melting earlier each year. The bears need the ice to reach their hunting grounds.

At the start of the book, we read about the sea otter. We heard how the loss of sea otters caused problems for kelp forests. Luckily, sea otters did not die out. But we must remember the story. It will remind us to protect natural habitats and food webs. Any break down in these complex connections will affect humans as well as other living things.

GLOSSARY

algae (AL jee) — most algae are tiny, plant-like living things, seaweeds are also algae

caiman (KAY muhn) — a kind of crocodile found in South America

caribou (KA ri boo) — a large mammal of the deer family, caribou are related to reindeer

decomposers (dee kuhm PO zurs) — living things such as fungi and bacteria that get food by breaking down the remains of plants or animals

diatoms (DYE at uhms) — a kind of plankton that have a glass-like shell around their bodies

dinoflagellates (DYE noh fla juh luhts) — a type of plankton that have long, whiplike flagella (tails) on their bodies

energy (EN ur jee) — the ability to do work, iIt is measured in joules

environment (en VYE ruhn muhnt) — the natural world of the land, oceans, and air

extinct (ek STINGKT) — when a particular kind of animal or plant dies out completely

herbivore (HUR buh vor) — an animal that eats only plant food

joule (jool) — a unit for measuring energy or work done

minerals (MIN ur uhl) — simple chemicals found in the ground

nitrates (NYE trayts) — chemicals containing the elements nitrogen and oxygen

nutrients (NOO tree hunts) — simple substances that animals need for food

omnivore (OM nuh vor) — an animal that eats a mixture of animal and plant foods

phytoplankton (FYE toh plangk tuhn) — plankton that can make their own food, as plants do

plankton (PLANGK tuhn) — microscopic and very small living things that drift with the ocean currents

predator (PRED uh tur) — an animal that catches and eats other animals

primary consumer (PRYE muh ree kuhn SOO mur) — any animal that eats plants or other producers

producer (pruh DOO sur) — a plant, or any other living thing that can make its own food

productivity (pruh DUHK tiv uh tee) — the amount of plant life that can grow in a particular environment

scavenger (SKAV uhn jur) — an animal that feeds on dead and rotting animals or other kinds of waste

secondary consumer (SEK uhn der ee kuhn SOO mur) — an animal whose main food is primary consumers

species (SPEE sheez) — a group of very similar animals that can breed together to produce healthy offspring

tertiary consumer (TUR shuh ree kuhn SOO mur) — an animal whose main food is secondary consumers

FURTHER INFORMATION

Books

Food Chains and Webs. Lewis Parker. Perfection Learning, 2005.

Life in a Kelp Forest. Mary Jo Rhodes and David Hall. Children's Press, 2006.

The World of Food Chains with Max Axiom, Super Scientist. Liam O'Donnell. Capstone Press, 2007.

Who Eats Who in City Habitats? Robert Snedden. North Mankato, Minnesota; Smart Apple Media, 2006. One of a series of books. Others cover food chains in grasslands, rainforests, deserts, rivers and lakes, and the seashore.

Websites to visit

www.pbs.org/edens/etosha/feedme.htm
This site takes a close look at the animal life in the Etosha National Park in southern Africa, and the food chains that they rely upon.

http://ecokids.earthday.ca/pub/eco_info/topics/frogs/ chain_reaction/index.cfm#
This activity allows you to try and build a food chain.

**http://curriculum.calstatela.edu/courses/builders/lessons/
less/biomes/introbiomes.html**
This site looks at food chains in different climates of
the world.

**www.bbc.co.uk/nature/blueplanet/webs/flash/
main_game.shtml**
BBC Nature.
Find out how species interact with one another in a
coral reef.

http://www.kidsknowit.com/interactive-educational
Kidsknowit Network.
This site provides a free movie on the food chain and
tests your knowledge with an online quiz.

INDEX